T3-AME-162

What went into this book?

Days of toil without a break!

Nights without sleep!

No time to wash or bathe!

Hastily prepared limburger cheese sandwiches on onion rolls, washed down with garlic soup!

Work, work, work—until his clothes were damp with sweat!

Is it any wonder that

DON MARTIN COMES ON STRONG?

Buy this book, pay through the nose, and laugh yourself *scents-less!*

Copyright © 1971 by Don Martin and E. C. Publications, Inc.

All rights reserved

 SIGNET TRADEMARK REG. U.S. PAT. OFF. AND FOREIGN COUNTRIES
REGISTERED TRADEMARK—MARCA REGISTRADA
HECHO EN CHICAGO, U.S.A.

SIGNET, SIGNET CLASSICS, SIGNETTE, MENTOR AND PLUME BOOKS
are published *in the United States* by
The New American Library, Inc.,
1301 Avenue of the Americas, New York, New York 10019,
in Canada by The New American Library of Canada Limited,
81 Mack Avenue, Scarborough, 704, Ontario,
in the United Kingdom by The New English Library Limited,
Barnard's Inn, Holborn, London, E.C. 1, England.

FIRST PRINTING, JULY, 1971

5 6 7 8 9 10 11 12

PRINTED IN THE UNITED STATES OF AMERICA

CONTENTS

STAR STRUCK OVER BROOKLYN

It's March . . . 1938 . . . show time at the old Funke St. Theatre . . .

8

9

So it was **you** who helped me out, out there! I don't know who you are or where you came from, but how would you like to be part of a team in show business?!? We'll be **fantastic** together!! I can **see it now!!** We'll play all the **big class spots!!!**

...And now, ladies and gentlemen: direct from a fantastic engagement at the world-famous Hotel Waldorf-Astoria in Slime Rock, Utah...the management of the El Swanko Nightclub and Pizzeria is proud to present...**Larry Lore and Snyder Spider!!!**

15

Mr. Lore, my name is Busby Bezerkly, the big Hollywood producer.

You mean there's a place for us in Hollywood?

Yes, but quite frankly—well, Mr. Lore...I can't use the two of you!

I'm sorry Mr. Bezerkly but we **can't split up the act!** That's one **solemn promise** Snyder and I made to each other...that we would **never split up the act.** I can't allow Snyder Spider to go to Hollywood unless I'm included in the deal!

You're a real trouper, Snyder.

24

27

29

Snyder, I know I broke our solemn promise, but I'm **back** now!...We'll be a **team again**!... We'll do the old **act again**!...

44

ONE SPRING DAY

SALE
WRIST
WATCHES →

SHOOKA
SHOOKA
SHOOKA

TICK-TOCK
TICK-TOCK
TAKOONK

48

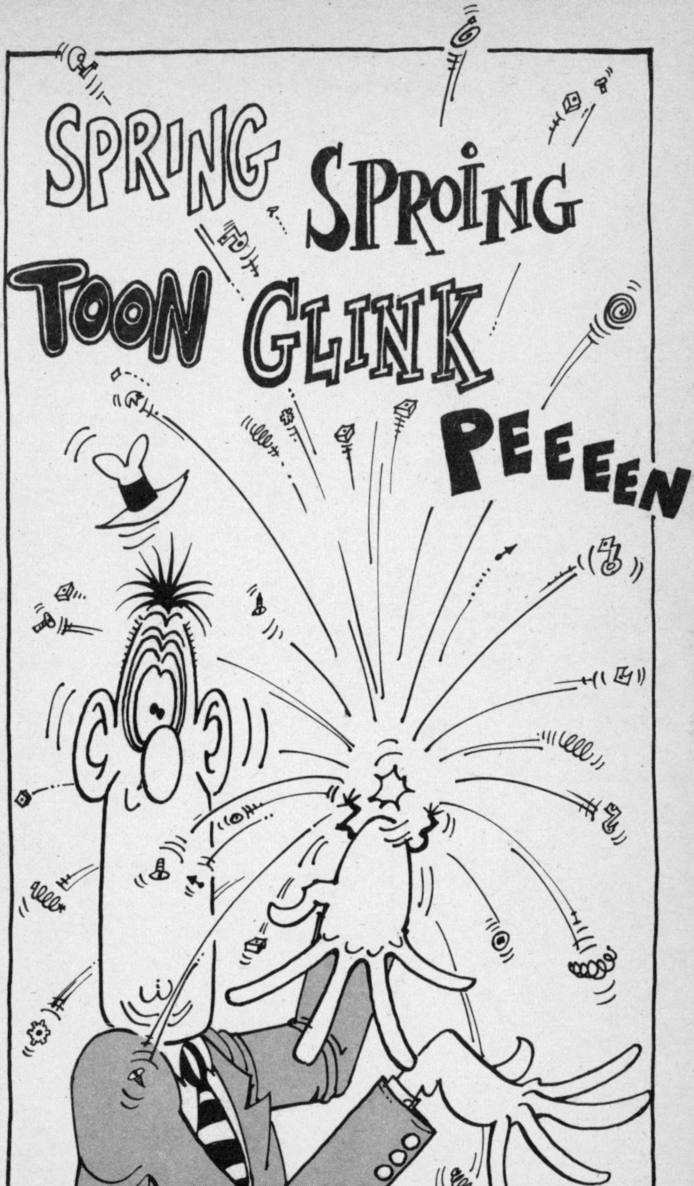
SPRING
SPROING
TOON
GLINK
PEEEEN

DRUMS ALONG THE UNION PACIFIC

PART ONE

The old West, where men were men, and women were women, and children were children, and terrible movies like this were unheard of . . .

By the way, you don't know where I can find a man named **Dirty Dan,** do you?
Maybe . . . and maybe not.
Does he live in this town?
Maybe . . . and maybe not.
Well, if you should see him, will you tell him a stranger is looking for him?
Maybe . . . and maybe not.
Can we have another fun chat like this again sometime?
Maybe . . . and . . .

64

Pattino, the cobbler, and his wife Ispido, spend many long hours in their cobbler shop, but no one ever comes in to have his shoes repaired. The fact that the front window says **"Bakery"** may have something to do with it ...

Meanwhile, down the street, lovely Spiga, the broom-maker's helper, finds her mind drifting toward thoughts of love ...

Her thoughts of love are for Mezluzzo,
a soldier who is off fighting, but
Mezluzzo's heart belongs to Isolando,
the bag-piper's niece...

Well, **whatever!** What we're **trying** to
get at is that the only way Isolando
returns Mezluzzo's love is by **not
accepting** delivery of his letters!

Mezluzzo, in a desperate attempt to find out why Isolando doesn't answer his letters, visits Vetrina, the gypsy . . .

72

Meanwhile, Spiga, the broom-maker's helper, still pines for Mezluzzo . . .

But in the meantime, the gypsy's spell takes effect and Isolando is mysteriously drawn to Mezluzzo . . .

Isolando and Mezluzzo lived together in ecstasy—which is just 20 miles south of Joy. Meanwhile, things got a lot worse for Spiga, who went from a broom-maker's helper to a *vacuum-cleaner-maker's helper* . . .

But in the little cobbler's shop, Pattino is very ill. Spillo, the physician is there . . .

That night Death visited the little cobbler shop and, like all Italian women, Ispido made Death a cup of coffee, some minestrone, and pastry . . .

Then . . . in a fantastic turn of events, Isolando is struck and killed by lightning while working in the cellar. It is while attending Pattino's funeral that Spiga comes face to face with Mezluzzo . . .

They stare at one another and for the first time Mezluzzo finds something in Spiga's eye that he never realized was there before.

Nancy Nice, Stewardess

Hi! I'm your **stewardess, Nancy Nice.** Before we attempt to take off, there are a few things I must tell you. First — I would like to explain what happens if the cabin should, for any reason, become depressurized.

93

. . . and GRAB FOR THAT JACKET!!! RIP-PULL-TEAR-TUG!!! ANYTHING to get it out of that tiny slot it's wedged into!!! Some people can NEVER get it out in time—so PULL!!!
UGH!
ECH!
EGH!

DRUMS ALONG THE UNION PACIFIC

PART TWO

. . . Meanwhile, across the street and 500 miles to the west . . . a stagecoach is riding across the plains . . .

111

We've been holding out for 7 days without **moving!** The boredom is driving me **crazy!** Nothing to **read**...nowhere to **go**...nothing! Just **nothing to do!!** And you just **stand there unconcerned!** How can you **do** that?!?

I'll explain it to you someday when we have some free time.

It's no use waiting here! I'm going out and **talk to those Indians!**

You're **out-of-your-mind!**

Don't try to **stop** me, Miss Amy! I **know** what I'm **doing!**

118

119

BEAUTY FROM THE **BEAST**

DING DING DING
DING DING
DING DING DING
DING DING

DIP-DIP-DIP-DIP

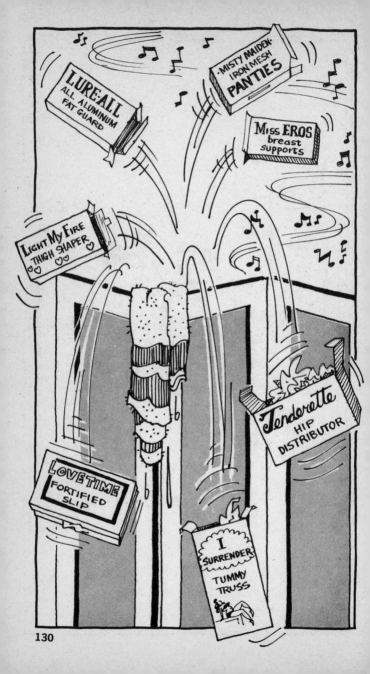

DINK·DINK·DINK·DINK

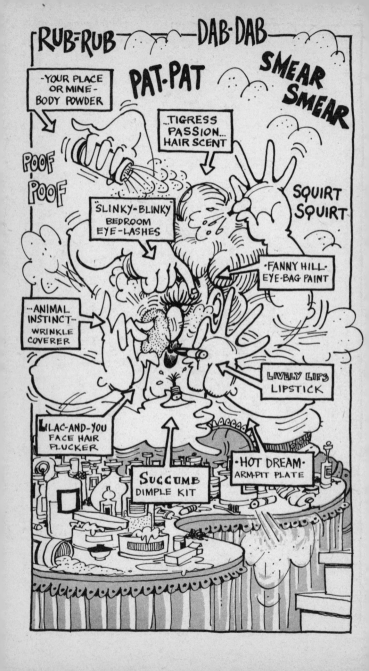

By golly, they're **right!**
I **can't** tell it from my own!

TIP-TIP-TIP

DRUMS ALONG THE UNION PACIFIC

PART THREE

... In the meantime, Glade is talking to old Pops Foster at the Foster Ranch ...

Well, Pops, I told you to move out of here while the gettin' was good! Now I'm cuttin' off **both your water rights!**

Both water rights?

Yeah! **Hot** and **cold!!**

ONE ARF-FUL DAY

147

SWIT SWIZZIT

ZAT
ZIP
ZOOP
ZAMP
ZAKO

KLIK

SKREEEEE

Welcome to Dog's Day Theatre playing famous movies of special interest to the canine set. Today's feature... **"Cat on a Hot Tin Roof"**.

PSSP!

I'm a few minutes early today! **Boy,** won't Wags be **glad to see me!**

CLIK
CLITTITY
CLIK

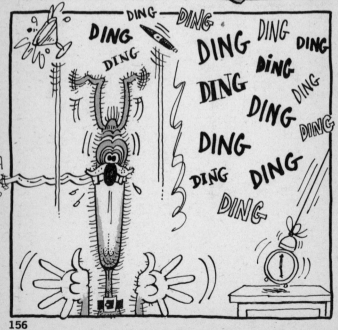

159

DRUMS ALONG THE UNION PACIFIC

PART FOUR

. . . Meanwhile, into the old West came the railroad . . . Dirty, dusty, noisy, and late! . . . just like today's railroads . . .

SKREEK

RUMBLE UMBLE

KALUNK

Taking his place with some of the world's best known make-believe crime fighters: people like Superman, Dick Tracy, Wonder Woman and J. Edgar Hoover . . . is the newest and most fearless hero of them all . . .

LANCE PARKERTIP

Noted Notary Public...

KLIKRUNK

175

Driver, I'm Lance Parkertip... Noted Notary Public. My card.
But this is a **laundry ticket.**
I know! I've written my name and address on the **back!** Listen, did you pick up a **woman** and a **dead man** from this address just a few minutes ago?
No, but I picked up a **man** and a **dead woman** from this address just a few minutes ago.
That's no help! **Wait a minute!!** Where did you **take** them?!?
To the Bye-Bye Funeral Home.
This could be a shot in the dark, but maybe there's going to be a **double burial!** Take me to the Bye-Bye Funeral Home and **hurry!!!**
·ACME LAUNDRY·
35 FONEBONE ST.
"WE TOIL TO CLEAN AWAY YOUR SOIL"

184

189

LANCE PARKERTIP—NOTED NOTARY PUBLIC

★ My Commission Expired ★

D.MARTiN